Jan Can Juggle

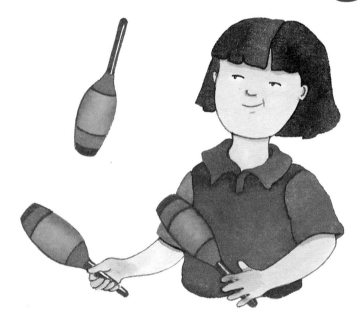

Written by Kate McGovern

Illustrated by Rosario Valderrama

Jan can juggle balls.

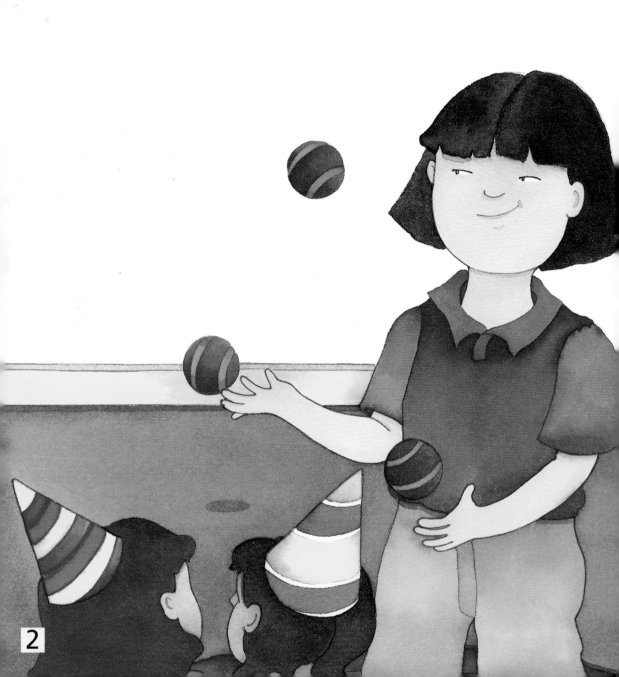

Jan can juggle jars.

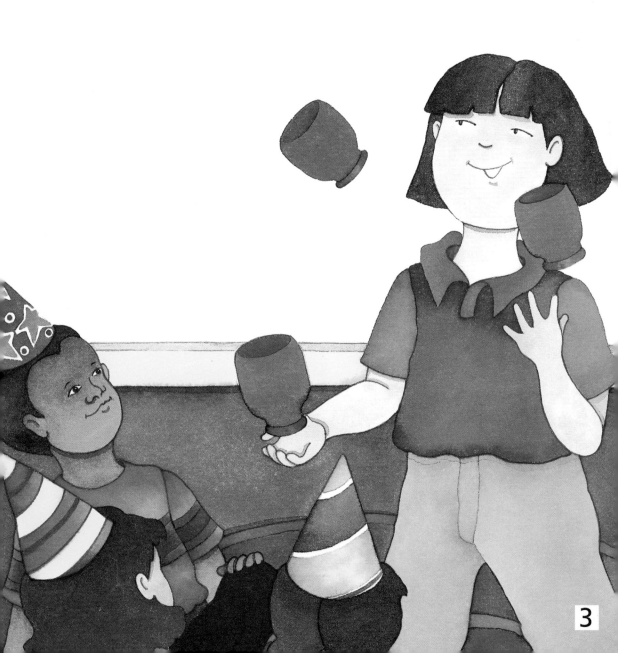

Jan can juggle jets.

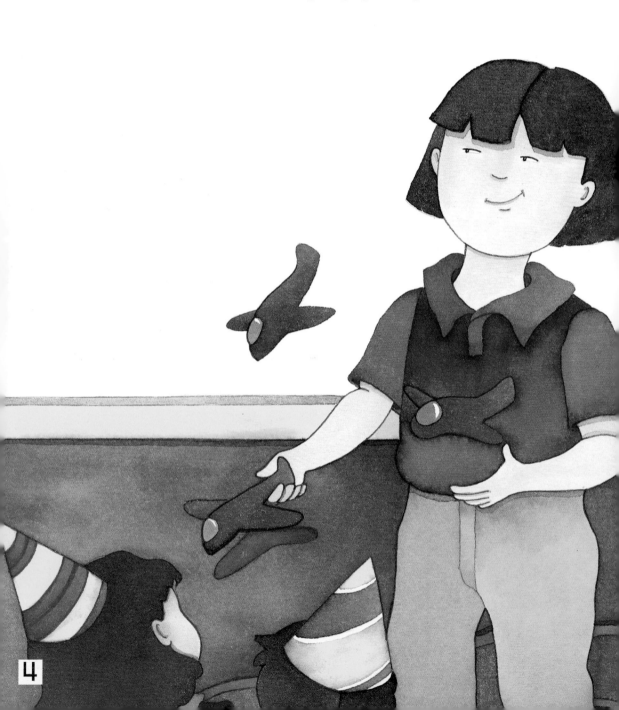

Jan can juggle stars.

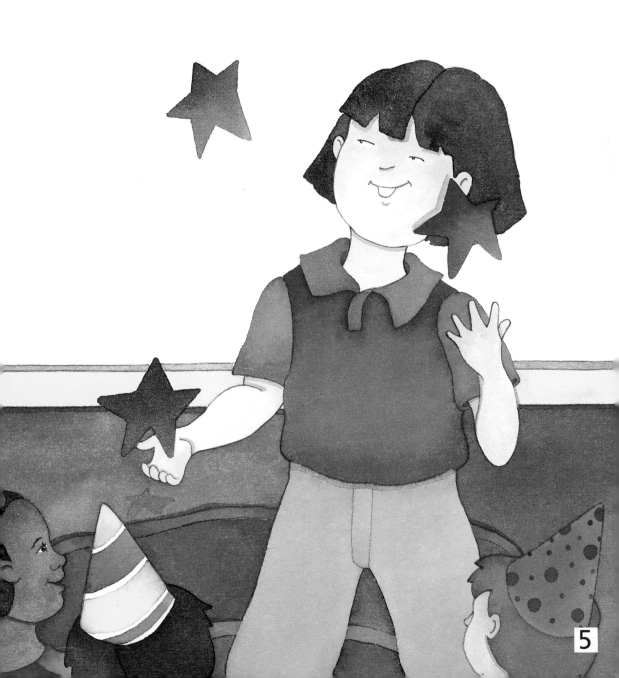

Jan can juggle apples.

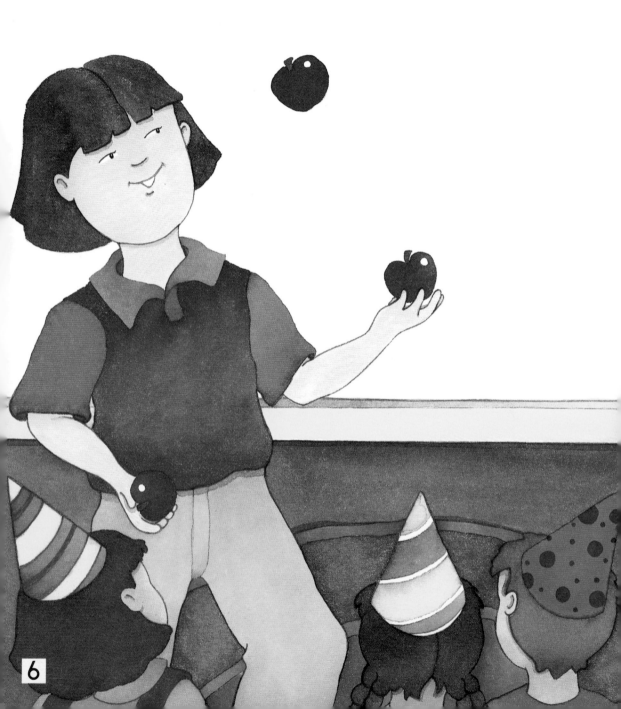

Jan can juggle eggs.

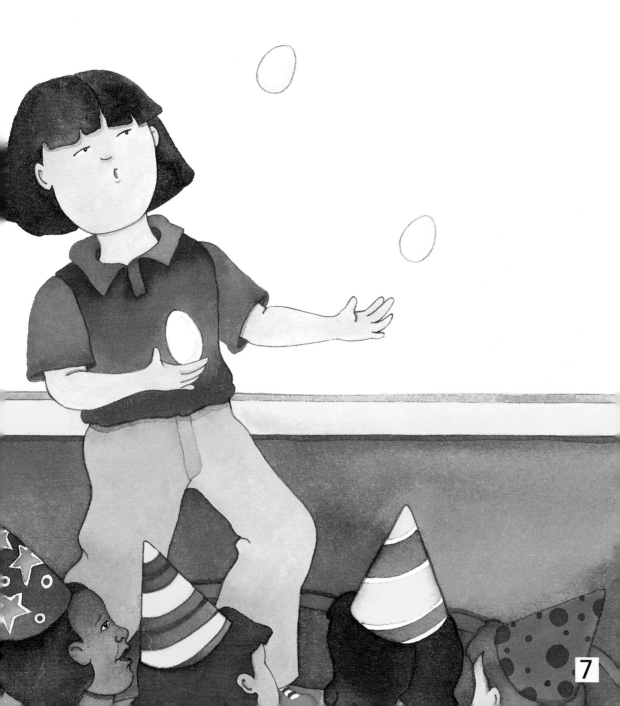

OOPS!